Royal Counsel

Copyright Harvey Christian Publishers Inc. 2019

All rights reserved. No part of this book may be reproduced or trans-mitted in any form or by any means, electronic or mechanical, including photocopying, recording, or by any information storage and retrieval system without written permission from the copyright owner, except for the inclusion of brief quotations in a review.

ISBN: 978-1-932774-04-7
Printed in USA

Cover Design by
Vladyslav Vitel
VladyslavVitel@gmail.com

Printed by
Lightning Source
La Vergne, TN 37086

Royal Counsel

Thirty-one
Stimulating Readings
on the Power of God's Word

Compiled by
Edwin and Lillian Harvey

Harvey Christian Publishers Inc.
449 Hackett Pike
Richmond, KY 40475
books@harveycp.com
www.harveycp.com

ROYALTY COUNSELS

He expounded unto them in all the Scriptures the things concerning himself (Luke 24:27).
And they said one to another, Did not our heart burn within us while he talked with us by the way, and while he opened to us the Scriptures (Luke 24:32)?
Then opened he their understanding, that they might understand the Scriptures (Luke 24:45).

The two disciples on the road to Emmaus had a most profitable journey. Their Companion and Teacher was the best of tutors; the interpreter, one of a thousand, in whom are hid all the treasures of wisdom and knowledge. The Lord Jesus condescended to become a Preacher of the Gospel, and He was not ashamed to exercise His calling before an audience of two persons.

Neither does He now refuse to become the Teacher of even one. Let us covet the company of so excellent an Instructor; for till He is made unto us wisdom, we shall never be wise unto salvation.

This unrivalled Tutor used as His class book the best of books. Although able to reveal fresh truth, He preferred to expound the old. He knew by His omniscience what was the most instructive way of teaching. By turning at once to Moses and the prophets, He showed us that the surest road to wisdom is not speculation, reasoning or reading human books, but meditation upon the Word of God. The readiest way to be spiritually rich in heavenly knowledge is to dig in this mine of diamonds, to gather pearls from the heavenly sea. When Jesus Himself sought to enrich others, He wrought in the quarry of Holy Scripture.

The favored pair were led to consider the best of subjects for Jesus spake of Jesus, and expounded the things concerning Himself. Here the diamond cut the diamond; and what could be more admirable? The Master of the house unlocked His own doors, conducted the guests to His table and placed His own dainties upon it.

He Who hid the treasure in the field, Himself guided the searchers to it. Our Lord would naturally discourse upon the sweetest of topics, and He could find none sweeter than His own person and work. With an eye to these, we should always search the Word. Oh, for grace to study the Bible with Jesus as both our Teacher and our lesson!
—*C. H. Spurgeon.*

>Divine Instructor, gracious Lord,
>Be Thou forever near;
>Teach us to love Thy sacred Word
>And view the Savior there.
>—*Anne Steele.*

C. T. Studd, during the first eighteen months of his missionary career in China was much alone with God and His Word. In his life story we discover what use he made of this time: "The outstanding lesson which he learnt during this period was to become a man of one Book. From this time onward it became a principle of his life to read the Bible, almost to the exclusion of other books, marking it copiously, and receiving it in the attitude of a little child, in simple dependence upon the Holy Spirit to illuminate the Word to him.

"Thus, living in direct communion with God through the Spirit and the Word, he never afterwards felt the need of conventions or other help from man to sustain and guide his spiritual life. He had learned the secret of walking with God alone."

Reading: Luke 24: 13-48.

CARGOES OF RICHES

The Lord shall open unto thee his good treasure (Deut. 28:12).
I love thy commandments above gold, yea, above fine gold
(Psa. 119:127).
More to be desired are they than gold, yea, than much fine gold
(Psa. 19:10).

Every book in the Bible is a revelation of the Lord Jesus Christ. I assure you that I find in every passage, even the driest, such cargoes of God's riches that I have not time to unload them, and there they lie at the wharf of my poor broken being, and I long for the hands, and the power, and the skill to take them into my soul.—*C. A. Fox.*

O thou Bible! holy Book of wonders! What more can we need, when He Who bears "the key of David," opens up to us thy treasures? Where is the darkness which thy light will not dispel? Where the emptiness which thy tree of life will not satisfy? Where is the thirst which thy living streams will not quench? Where the mountains which cannot be ascended, when we have with us thy rod and staff?

> Would it not be a foolish thing
> To die of thirst, with this clear spring
> Of living water at my feet?
> To starve when there is bread and meat
> And wine before me on the board,
> A table spread by my dear Lord?
> And would we think he had much sense
> Who hoarded only copper pence
> When at his feet, and all around
> Were diamonds sparkling on the ground?

The Lord I love went on ahead
To make a home for me. He said
He would come back again, and He,
O gracious love, He wrote to me!
He knew I was so weak and blind
And foolish that I could not find
The road alone. He told me things
That all earth's wise men and its kings
Have never guessed, yet I foreknow
If I but read His Word. And oh,
Such depths of love on every sheet!
My soul is trembling at His feet.
—*Martha Snell Nicholson.*

Next to the joy of winning a soul, is that of discovering a nugget of pure gold in the Bible (incidentally, both joys are often bound together). Not much equipment is needed—just a Bible, a concordance, possibly a Bible dictionary, pen and ink, and above all a will to study, a willingness to work. The decision to put this before some other things will ensure that the Bible ever afterwards will be a rich mine of ever-fresh delight.

The Master is here and He is asking us 20th century Christians, "How readest thou?" "Understandest thou what thou readest?" We who are young must be diligent and we who are older and have become negligent of our Bibles, must recover the joy, the early joy of Bible study! The Book demands something better than a careless reading, and as touching its Author and subject, "He is worthy, then give Him nothing less than the best."—*Fred Mitchell.*

Reading: Psalms 19.

VIBRANT WITH LIFE

The words that I speak unto you, they are spirit, and they are life (John 6:63).
The word of God is not bound (2 Tim. 2:9).
The dead shall hear the voice of the Son of God; and they that hear shall live (John 5:25).

An old Professor of biology used to hold a little brown seed in his hand. "I know just exactly the composition of this seed. It has in it nitrogen, hydrogen and carbon. I know the exact proportions. I can make a seed that will look exactly like it. But if I plant my seed it will come to naught; its elements will simply be absorbed in the soil. If I plant the seed God made, it will become a plant, because it contains the mysterious principle which we call 'the life principle.' The Bible looks like other books. We cannot understand altogether its marvelous power. Planted in good ground it shows that it has the life principle in itself; it brings forth spiritual fruitage."
—*Message from God.*

"The words He speaks are spirit and life." Wherever they fall, though into dull and lifeless soil, they begin to breed life, and produce results like themselves. . . . If only those words, spoken from the lips of Christ, be allowed to work in the conscience, there will be forthwith the stir of life.

The Word of God is active, *i.e.,* energetic. Beneath its spell the blind see, the deaf hear, the paralyzed are nerved with new energy, the dead stir in their graves and come forth. There are few things more energetic than life. Put a seed into the fissure of a rock, and it will split it in twain from top to bottom.

Though walls and rocks and ruins impede the course of the seedling, yet it will force its way to the light, and air and rain. And when the Word of God enters the heart, it is not as a piece of furniture or lumber. It asserts itself and strives for mastery, and compels men to give up sin; to make up long-standing feuds; to restore ill-gotten gains; to strive to enter into the strait gate. "Now ye are pruned," said our Lord, "through the word that I have spoken unto you." The words of Christ are His winnowing-fan, with which He is wont to purge His floor, whether in the heart or the world.—*F. B. Meyer.*

> He speaks and listening to His voice,
> New life the dead receive;
> The mournful, broken hearts rejoice,
> The humble poor believe.
> —*Charles Wesley.*

"The Word of God is not bound." It is a seed; a living seed. It grows. It yields a harvest. One sacred text begets another. God speaks; but the Infinite cannot say everything in a sentence, or pack His whole revelation into one soul. He speaks at sundry times and in different ways. He magnifies His Word, and makes it honorable, by repetitions, retranslations, revised versions, re-announcements, victories. Isaiah repeats Micah, Luther repeats the Psalmist, Carey repeats the prophet, and so the Word of the Lord has free course and is multiplied.—*John Clifford.*

We are supernatural people, born again by a supernatural birth, kept by a supernatural power, sustained on supernatural food, taught by a supernatural Teacher from a supernatural Book.—*Hudson Taylor.*

Reading: Luke 8:4-15; Acts 10:34-48.

FEED ON GOD'S THOUGHTS

Blessed is the man that walketh not in the counsel of the ungodly. . . But his delight is in the law of the Lord: and in his law doth he meditate day and night . . . he bringeth forth his fruit in his season . . . and whatsoever he doeth shall prosper (Psa. 1:1-3).

The first thing and the last thing to be studied is the Bible. The doctor may know all about law and art, history and theology, but if he is unacquainted with his medical books he will be a failure as a doctor. The lawyer may have devoured libraries, traveled the wide world over, and become a walking encyclopedia and dictionary, but if he is unacquainted with his law books, as a lawyer he will be a failure.

So the worker for souls may read ten thousand books, may be able to quote poetry by the yard, may be acquainted with all the facts of science and history, and may even be a profound theologian, but unless he is a diligent student of the Bible, he will not permanently succeed as a soul-winner. **He must become full of the thoughts of God.** He must eat the Word, and digest it, and turn it into spiritual blood and bone, and muscle and nerve and sinew, until he becomes, as someone has said, "a living Bible, eighteen inches wide by six feet long, bound in human skin."—*Samuel L. Brengle.*

When Goforth was asked by young missionaries as to the secret of his power in winning converts, his reply was: "Because I just give God a chance to speak to souls through His own Word."

The third secret of Mr. Moody's power, or the third reason why God used D. L. Moody, was because **he was a deep and practical student of the Word of God.** Nowadays it is often said of D. L. Moody that he was not a student. I wish to say that he was a student; most emphatically he was a student. He was not a student of psychology; he was not a student of anthropology—I am very sure he would not have known what that word meant; he was not a student of biology; he was not a student of philosophy; he was not even a student of theology, in the technical sense of the term; but he was a student, a profound and practical student of the one Book that is more worth studying than all other books in the world put together; he was a student of the Bible. Every day of his life, I have reason for believing, he arose very early in the morning to study the Word of God, way down to the close of his life. Mr. Moody used to rise about four o'clock in the morning to study the Bible. He would say to me: "If I am going to get in any study, I have got to get up before the other folks get up"; and he would shut himself up in a remote room in his house, alone with his God and his Bible.

If you wish to get an audience and wish to do that audience some good, study, **study,** STUDY the one Book, and preach, **preach,** PREACH the one Book, and teach, **teach,** TEACH the one Book, the Bible, the only Book that contains God's Word, and the only Book that has power to gather and hold and bless the crowds for any great length of time.—*R. A. Torrey.*

Reading: Psalms 1; Psalms 119:97-104;
2 Chronicles 17:7-10.

COPYRIGHTED IN HEAVEN

The word of the Lord endureth for ever (1 Pet. 1:25).
Concerning thy testimonies, I have known of old that thou hast founded them for ever (Psa. 119:152).
For ever, O Lord, thy word is settled in heaven (Psa. 119:89).

"For ever, O Lord, Thy word is settled in heaven." This was Luther's maxim, inscribed on the walls of his chamber and embroidered on his robe. It means that the Word of God is established in Heaven—far above and beyond the reach of all disturbing causes, as the stars are beyond the reach of man's watering pot, and cannot be quenched by the ocean spray.—*A. T. Pierson.*

> Almighty Lord, the sun shall fail,
> The moon forget her nightly tale,
> And deepest silence hush on high
> The radiant chorus of the sky.
>
> But, fixed for everlasting years,
> Unmoved amid the wreck of spheres,
> Thy Word shall shine in cloudless day
> When Heaven and earth have passed away.
> —*Grant.*

The Bible is one of the solid facts of Christianity. What it is, is not affected by what men think of it. Changing opinions about the Bible do not change the Bible. Whatever the Bible was, the Bible is. And what it is, it has always been. It is not men's thoughts about the Bible that judge it. It is the Bible which judges men and their thoughts. It has nothing to fear but ignorance and neglect. And the Church need have no other fear on its account. The Bible will take care of itself if the Church will distribute it and get it read.
—*Robert E. Speer.*

The scripture cannot be broken (John 10:35).

The Bible needs no defense from men. Exiled, it has created a new kingdom and shifted the center and balance of power. Carried away captive, it has broken down rival altars, and overthrown false gods, till the right of way has been accorded to it by friend and foe. . . .

Burned in the public square by the public executioner it has risen sphinx-like and floated away in triumph, waving the smoke of its own funeral pyre as a flag of victory. Scourged from city to city, it has gone through the capitals of the civilized world, leaving behind it a trail of light attesting its divine authority.

—*Bishop Charles Fowler.*

This royal writing "may no man reverse." The King Himself cannot reverse it, for He changes not; "He **cannot** lie," "He **cannot** deny Himself," for unchangeable truth is not only an essential attribute, but the very essence of His Deity. This one great **"cannot"** is the security for all that He "can" and will do.

—*Frances Ridley Havergal.*

An infidel lecturer in England was once asked, "Why can't you let the Bible alone, if you don't believe it?" The honest reply was at once made, "Because the Bible won't let me alone!"

Reading: Psalms 78:1-8; Psalms 119:89-96; 1 Peter 1:9-25.

EXPLORE THE RARELY VISITED NOOKS

All Scripture is given by inspiration of God (2 Tim. 3:16).
One jot or one title (the smallest letter in the Greek and Hebrew alphabet) shall in no wise pass from the law, till all be fulfilled. Whosoever therefore shall break one of these least commandments, and shall teach men so, he shall be called the least in the kingdom of heaven (Matt. 5: 18,19).
He expounded unto them in ALL the Scriptures (Luke 24:27).

It seems as if God wanted to encourage and stimulate close, minute, diligent, thorough and loving study of the Holy Scriptures, and to do this He has put many of the very best things of His Word in these obscure and rarely visited nooks and along what appear to be uninviting bypaths to reward those who press with enthusiastic eagerness into all ways in quest of even the smallest bit of divine truth . . . .

There are whole sections of the Scriptures which are little more than unknown country to most people. This is true very largely of the prophetical books, especially of the minor prophets. But in this neglect we are sore losers. No part of the Bible is desert; no part is even sterile. If there are portions that are bare on the surface, they contain rich mineral wealth which we can find by digging down through the rugged crust. At least it is certain that there is not one chapter of the Bible without its tufts of grass or its nuggets of gold. But the best things in the holy Book, like all the best things, must be sought for, and sought for eagerly. Careless, superficial reading will never find much that is very precious or helpful. God has hidden away in obscure nooks, in unattractive chapters, many of the finest things in His Word; and we can get them only by pressing our quest into every bypath and into all crannies.—*J. R. Miller.*

Grace puts within my reach the Written Word,
    Love says, "Awake, be up betimes and read."
Hope beckons, saying, "Here is store indeed
To meet the longings in thy spirit stirred."

Faith whispers, "Let the still small voice be heard,
    The voice of One Who with thy soul can plead,
    And at the Throne of Mercy intercede,
Lest in thy pride or haste the truth be slurred."

    "Angel of patience, has thou naught to say?"
    "Child, thou hast need of me the live-long day,
He who would grasp the Scriptures as a whole
Must bring to study them a yielded soul;
    And searching deeper he will this discern,
The more he studies, there is more to learn."
                            —*Edith E. Trusted.*

    I am fascinated with the conciseness of that Book. Every word is packed full of truth. Every sentence is double-barreled. Every paragraph is like an old banyan tree, with a hundred roots and a hundred branches. The Bible was not merely made to sell; it was not presented merely for a trifling and temporary effect. It is a great arch; pull out one stone and it all comes down. There has never been a pearl-diver who could gather up one half of the treasures in any verse. John Halsebach, of Vienna, for twenty-one years, every Sabbath expounded to his congregation the first chapter of the Book of Isaiah, and yet did not get through with it. Nine-tenths of all the good literature of this age is merely the Bible diluted.—*De Witt Talmage.*

Reading: Joshua 8:30-35; Acts 18:24-28; 1 Timothy 4:6-16.

TWENTY YEARS OF DAILY PROMISES

His divine power hath given unto us all things that pertain unto life and godliness, through the knowledge of him that hath called us to glory and virtue: Whereby are given unto us exceeding great and precious promises: that by these ye might be partakers of the divine nature, having escaped the corruption that is in the world through lust (2 Pet. 1:3-4).
For he is faithful that promised (Heb. 10:23).
There hath not failed one word of all his good promise
(1 Kings 8:56).

If you were to claim a promise every single day for more than twenty years you could still not exhaust the fund of God's promises to man. Everk R. Storms, Editor of the *Gospel Banner*, has made some recent computations from a study of the promises and he says there are 7,487 promises given by God to man. Andrew Bonar said once that Caleb lived for forty years upon one promise: what could we not do upon 7,487? Below are a few of Editor Storms' interesting figures:

    8,810 promises are in the Bible
    1,104 are in the New Testament.
    Isaiah, Jeremiah and Ezekiel have slightly over 1,000 promises each.
    Titus has no promises at all.
    Seventeen other books contain less than ten promises each.
    Of the 8,810 promises there are eight different kinds.
    7,487 promises given by God to man.
    991 promises made by one man to another.
    290 made by man to God (most of them in the Psalms).
    28 made by angels.
    9 made by the devil.
    2 made by an evil spirit.
    2 by God the Father to the Son.
    1 by man to an angel.

Psalm 37 has 43 precious promises.
Deuteronomy 28 has 133 promises.

The same writer says: "There promises are ours for the asking. They are waiting for us to test and prove them. We go to church and sing, 'Standing on the promises,' but most of us are sitting on them."

> Take to yourself the promises,
> Found in His Holy Word,
> Bring to your mind His messages,
> Have faith that you are heard,
> When in your need you pray to Him,
> To strengthen you just there,
> Claim His most precious promises,
> You'll find God answers prayer.
> —*Clara Simpson.*

John Bunyan thought much of the promises of God. "I tell thee, friend," he said, "there are some promises that the Lord hath helped me to lay hold of in Jesus Christ . . . that I would not have out of the Bible for as much gold and silver as can lie between York and London piled up to the stars."

Reading: Psalms 37.

THE BIBLE—A FRIEND IN NEED

I am afflicted very much: quicken me, O Lord, according unto thy word (Psa. 119:107).
It is good for me that I have been afflicted; that I might learn thy statutes (Psa. 119:71).

When did the Bible cease to care for men? When did the Bible ever lose itself in ideal contemplation, and withdraw itself from the line of human want, and sorrow and pain, and wound, and helplessness? This is the one Book in the library that sits up all night with us, that goes the whole road of life step for step with us, and that is tenderest when we are sorest, mightiest when we most realize our own helplessness.—*Joseph Parker.*

Are we voyagers upon a troubled and dangerous sea? Here is a chart by which to steer in safety to the happy shores. Are we soldiers, beset with foes and required to endure the shocks of battle? This is an armory from which all needed weapons may be drawn at will, and by the right use of which we may win our way to immortal triumph. Are we pilgrims and strangers, worn and weary in our search for the home from which we are exiles? In this Book, gush out the pure, fresh waters of life, the cooling shades from the Rock of salvation appear, and the guiding word is heard from pilgrims in advance, to cheer and encourage us till we reach our Father's mansion.

Indeed, it is beyond the power of language to express the excellence and richness of spiritual treasure which we have in this holy Book. It is the miraculous cruse of the Shunamites which never exhausts. It is the wand of Moses which swallows the serpents of life, and parts the sea of trouble, and brings forth waters in the thirsty wilderness. It is the ladder of Jacob on which our spirits ascend to commune with God and angels.—*Joseph A. Seiss.*

Could I have found Thy Word
My bulwark
If shipwreck had not overtaken me?
For words I spoke by rote
In chaos and in flood tide rescued me.
What passed before
Was empty rhetoric,
Sincere but untried truth,
All glibly said,
Till I had need
For more than speech.

"Send safety and salvation!"
In wordless grief I prayed.
And, stronger than the ship
Of self-sufficiency,
Thy Word
My shipwrecked soul
Brought safe to shore.
—*Ruth T. Spinnanger.*

On most occasions of very sharp pressure or trial, some word of Scripture has come home to me as if borne on angel's wings. Many could I recollect.—*Gladstone.*

Reading: Psalms 119:65-72, 105-112, 153-160.

THE ROYAL TUTOR

The secret things belong unto the Lord our God: but those things which are revealed belong unto us (Deut. 29:29).
God hath revealed them unto us by his Spirit: for the Spirit searcheth all things, yea, the deep things of God (1 Cor. 2:10).

    Remember that the words (of the Bible) are Spirit, and can only be profitably received by the teaching of the Spirit. Thus reading, and thus praying, you have a Scriptural warrant to expect that He Who wrote the Bible will tell you words in secret which shall not only be life to your own soul, but which, when you proclaim them as you have opportunity to others, shall be to the glory of God and the good of men.—*Brownlow North.*

> Do men dare to call Thy Scripture—
>   Mystic forest, unillumined nook?
> If it be so, O my spirit!
>   Then let Christ arise on thee, and look
> With the long lane of His sunlight
>   Shall be cut the forest of His Book.
>   —*Unknown.*

    The Bible is a sealed Book to unspiritual people, but when the Comforter comes it is unsealed and opened, and its wondrous meaning made clear. I read recently of a lad who could not read, receiving the baptism of the Holy Ghost. Then he got his unsaved sister to read the Bible to him, and he explained it to her. The Holy Ghost in him enabled him to understand what the Holy Ghost in holy men of old enabled them to write. Only the Holy Ghost can help men to understand His Book.—*Samuel L. Brengle.*

    Finney used to get up at four o'clock in the morning to read his Bible until eight. He says, "My days were spent, as far as I could get time, in searching the Scriptures. I read nothing else all that winter but my Bible, and a great deal of it seemed new to me. Again the Lord took me as it were from Genesis to Revelation. He let me see the connection of things, the promises, the threatenings, the prophecies and their fulfillment; and, indeed, the whole Scripture seemed to me all ablaze with light."

The Holy Spirit alone can teach us about our state by nature, show us the need of a Savior, enable us to believe in Christ, explain to us the Scriptures, help us in preaching, etc. It was my beginning to understand this latter point in particular which had a great effect on me; for the Lord enabled me to put it to the test of experience, by laying aside commentaries, and almost every other book, and simply reading the Word of God and studying it. The result of this was, that the first evening I shut myself into my room, to give myself to prayer and meditation over the Scriptures, I learned more in a few hours than I had done during a period of several months previously. But the particular difference was, that I received real strength for my soul in doing so. I now began to try by the test of the Scriptures the things which I had learned and seen, and found that only those principles, which stood the test, were really of value.—*George Müller.*

Reading: 1 Corinthians 2.

THE BOOK THAT FITS ME!

All these things happened unto them for ensamples: and they are written for our admonition (1 Cor. 10:11).
In thy book all my members were written. . . . How precious also are thy thoughts unto me, O God! how great is the sum of them (Psa. 139:16-17)!

    The Book of God is pre-eminently the Book of man. It is God's message to man—written with omniscient knowledge of man's nature and need, with infinite wisdom as to the best way to meet all man's problems, and with perfect love to assure a sympathetic and gracious ministry to his fallen condition. Hence we may expect to find not only that everything in this Book serves an end in man, but that everything in man is served by something in the Book.
    This we account a wonderful feature in this most wonderful Book; that it exactly finds man's deepest need and as exactly fits into it. It pierces to the mysterious realm—the dividing asunder of soul and body.—*A. T. Pierson.*

    A missionary once gathered some shepherds together to read the Bible and preach to them. He read to them the tenth chapter of John. The men listened intently; they had never heard the words before. One of them asked the missionary what he was reading. He replied that it was the Bible, the Word of God.
    The shepherd said, "Why, that's a sheep book."
    The man recognized that the Bible had a special message for shepherds, and he was right. No matter what sort of work a man is engaged in, the Bible has something to say about it and something to say to him.—*Selected.*

    Arthur Hallam said that the Bible proves itself God's Book, because it is man's Book, fitting every turn and curve of the human heart. He who has fed his own spiritual life through its pages will have no doubt about offering it as the word of life to hungry souls.

> Holy Bible! Book divine!
> Precious treasure! Thou art mine!
> Mine to tell me whence I came;
> Mine to teach me what I am;
> Mine to chide me when I rove;
> Mine to show a Savior's love;
> Mine art thou to guide my feet;
> Mine to judge, condemn, acquit;
> Mine to comfort in distress,
> In the Holy Spirit bless;
> Mine to show by living faith
> Man can triumph over death;
> Mine to tell of joys to come,
> And the rebel sinner's doom.
> —Anon.

Oh matchless and glorious Book, the Word of God to men—to us; revealing not only God, but ourselves; explaining moods for which we had no cipher; touching us as no other book can, and in moments when all voices beside wax faint and still; telling facts which we had not been able to discover, but which we instantly recognize as truth; the bread of the soul; the key of life, disclosing more depths as we climb higher in Christian experience. We have tested thee too long to doubt that thou art what Jesus said thou wast, the indispensable and precious gift of God.—*F. B. Meyer.*

Come, see a Book that has told me all that ever I did in my life; is not this the Book of God?—*T. Halyburton.*

Reading: Deuteronomy 11.

ROYAL STANDARDS

Keep my commandments, and live (Prov. 7:2).
Have I not written to thee excellent things in counsels and knowledge; That I might make thee know the certainty of the words of truth (Prov. 22:20-21).
Sanctify them through thy truth; thy word is truth (John 17:17).

We would refuse to live in a standardless community. Our whole way of life is built on standards—standards of weight; standards of measurement; standards of food purity; standards of housing; standards of hygiene; standards for road users—standards, standards, standards. We live sanely and securely because of standards. Remove them, and in twenty-four hours there would be pandemonium—chaos.

And there is chaos today in the most vital departments of our lives, because moral and spiritual standards have become obscured. We have not flung our Bibles away, but we take the easy way of conforming to man's opinions and relegating the Bible to the attic of our minds to be treasured as an antique, out of fashion for everyday use.

We may hold any opinions we please when nothing is involved. But when it comes to something vital, we must have the truth or we miss everything.

This is clearly shown by the story of the man who rushed to the ticket office and pantingly asked, "When does the 5:30 train leave?" "At 5:30, of course," was the reply. "Well," said the passenger, "whose clock am I to go by? It's 5:27 by the church clock, 5:25 by the post office clock, and your station clock tells me it's 5:32." "You can go by any clock you like," answered the other, "but you can't go by the 5:30 train for it has already gone."

May we Christians take heed to His Word so that we do not miss God's train of deliverance and blessing because we have gone by someone's imperfect human time-piece.

Thy Word is Truth! Thy Word is Light
   Undimmed by cloud or age:
Thy Son of Love—clear, spotless, bright—
   Gilds every glowing page.

Thy Word is Truth! 'Tis here Thy grace
   Shines forth amid the night:
A star to guide our wandering race,
   By faith, to perfect sight.

Thy Word is Truth! Men come and go;
   Age follows mortal youth;
Thy Word, Thyself, no change can know,
   Both are Eternal Truth.
                —*William Luff.*

    I cannot too greatly emphasize the importance and value of Bible Study. It is more important than ever before, in these days of uncertainties, when men and women are apt to decide questions from the standpoint of expedience rather than the eternal principles laid down by God Himself.—*John Wanamaker.*

    He who sets his own copy keeps writing worse and worse.
                                    —*Frances E. Willard.*

Reading: Malachi 2:1-17, 3:6-15.

DIVINE AUTHORSHIP

I have given unto them the words which thou gavest me; and they have received them (John 17:8).
I have given them thy word (John 17:14).
The Lord gave the word; great was the company of those that published it (Psa. 68:11).

Think what it is, always to have the Book of God! It comes from Him; He inspired holy men to write it; one Spirit breathes through it all; it is God Himself Who speaks to us in it. But He speaks by means of a **Book**. A voice is heard, and may quickly be forgotten; a message is received, and may easily pass from the mind; but a book remains. God has given us a **Book**, His own Book.

Thus He speaks to us. Not a day, but we may hear His voice. We have but to open the pages, and there we find the words of the living God. And this Book may be in every house; and every person may have it for his own.—*Rev. F. Bourdillon.*

My friends, this is no common Book. It is not the sayings of the sages of Greece; here are not the utterances of philosophers of past ages. If these words were written by man, we might reject them; but, oh, let me think the solemn thought, that this Book is God's handwriting—that these words are from the hills of Heaven. Let me look at its letters; they flash glory on my eye. Let me read the chapters; they are big with meaning and mysteries unknown. Let me turn over the prophecies; they are pregnant with unthought-of wonders. Oh, Book of books! And wast thou written by my God? Then will I bow before thee. Oh! tremble, tremble, lest any of you despise it; mark its authority, for it is the Word of God.—*Charles H. Spurgeon.*

> Thine, Thine, this Book, though given
> In man's poor human speech,
> Telling of things unseen, unheard,
> Beyond all human reach.
> —*Horatius Bonar.*

What finite mind can estimate its worth or describe the attention and reverence with which it ought to be regarded? The ancient Greeks had one sentence which they believed to have descended from Heaven. And to evince their gratitude and veneration for this gift, they caused it to be engraven, in letters of gold, on the front of their most sacred and magnificent temple. We, more favored, have not a sentence only, but a Volume which really descended from Heaven; and which, whether we consider its contents or its Author, ought to be indelibly engraven on the heart of every child of Adam. Its Author is the Author of our being; and it informs us, with the greatest clearness and precision, of everything necessary either to our present or future happiness; of everything, in fact, which its Author knows, the knowledge of which would be useful to us.—*Edward Payson.*

> Word of the everlasting God,
> Will of His glorious Son:
> Without Thee how could earth be trod,
> Or Heaven itself be won?

Reading: John 17.

REMIND GOD OF HIS PROMISES

And now, O Lord God, thou art that God, and thy words be true, and thou hast promised this goodness unto thy servant
(2 Sam. 7:28).
Lord God of Israel, there is no God like thee, in heaven above, or on earth beneath, who keeps covenant and mercy with thy servants that walk before thee with all their heart (1 Kings 8:23).

An old minister said to me early in my ministry, "Young man, learn to plead the promises of God in prayer."

That taught me the real secret of intercession. I have prayed differently ever since. Rather than lift my longing desires and aspirations to God in prayer, I learned to remind the Lord of His own promises. This gave me faith.

Is this not the very heart of being the Lord's Remembrancers—to remind God of His own Word? (Isa. 62:6). Prayer should take the size and shape of God's promises.—*Armin R. Gesswein.*

D. L. Moody says, "Tarry at a promise and God will meet you there. Take the promises of God. Let a man feed for a month on the promises of God, and he will not talk about his poverty, and how downcast he is, and what trouble he has day by day. You hear people say, 'Oh, my leanness! How lean I am!' My friends, it is not their leanness, it is their laziness! If you would only go from Genesis to Revelation, and see all the promises made by God to Abraham, to Isaac and to Jacob, to the Jews, and the Gentiles, and to all His people everywhere; if you would spend a month feeding on the precious promises of God, you would not go about with your heads hanging down like bulrushes, complaining how poor you are; but you would lift up your heads with confidence and proclaim the riches of His grace because you could not help it."

The evangelist, Gipsy Smith, tells of an interesting object lesson taught him by his father: When my father and my uncles were once holding meetings in a village, my father took me to a cherry-tree.

For the first time I thought he could not be sane. He stood under the cherry-tree, and held out his jacket, and cried, "Cherries, come down into my pocket!" After a time I thought I had better say, "Father, you must pluck them." "Ah, my dear," he said, "that is what I want you to see. I have heard you pray, night and morning, 'Lord, make me a good boy,' when God is just hanging all over and around you the cherries of His promises. All you have to do is to pluck them and claim them for your own. We must not be satisfied with merely asking God to help us. We must do our part by accepting and carrying out His commands."

>Behold the throne of grace;
>   The promise calls us near;
>There Jesus shows a smiling face,
>   And waits to answer prayer.
>
>My soul, ask what thou wilt,
>   Thou canst not be too bold;
>Since His own blood for thee He spilt,
>   What else can He withhold?
>   —*John Newton.*

Bring Christ's Word, Christ's promise, and Christ's sacrifice—His blood—with thee, and not one of Heaven's blessings can be denied thee.—*Adam Clarke.*

Reading: 1 Kings 8:20-56.

SOUL BATHING

Now ye are clean through the word which I have spoken unto you
 (John 15:3).
That he might sanctify and cleanse it with the washing of water by the word (Eph. 5:26).
Wherewithal shall a young man cleanse his way? By taking heed thereto according to thy word (Psa. 119:9).

After a few hours spent shopping or traveling you have inescapably become contaminated with the soil and grime of the city or town. The effects are clearly visible upon the face and hands as you view yourself in the mirror. So you refresh yourself with a thorough wash.

Likewise when mixing with the world, or even among Christian friends who do not bathe often in the Word, the soul comes home to relax only to see itself in the mirror of God's Word, begrimed by the filth of this world's opinions and groveling materialism. It must go for washing in the cleansing Word. "Now ye are clean through the Word I have spoken." Here standards of conduct and thinking are once again re-adjusted to God's; minds smudged with conversation, light and chaffy and sometimes even suggestive of moral filth, eyes that have of necessity seen much that is likely to contaminate the soul—all need the washing under God's Word.

> Weary and dusty from earth's contact, foul,
> I run to thee, O cleansing Word, unfailing;
> And bathed at thy blest fount of truth return
> To walk above earth's doubts and sins prevailing.
> —H. E. Forster.

Little Dickie hated washing up time. Whenever he saw the soap and water he screwed up his face. One day coming in with signs of dirt visibly present, his mother suggested another washing up time. Protesting violently, his mother said, "Why Dickie, don't you like to be clean?"

"Yes, mother," he sighed, almost in tears, "but can't you just dust me?"

There are many Christians like Dickie, who prefer a mere dusting up, instead of a good time around the Word. A quick glance at the Bible, a hurried dust-up with several verses or a promise, and they think they are clean.

Chrysostom, a saintly early Church Father, warns: "As people's bodies, when deprived of the benefit of the bath, become all full of dirt and filth, so also the soul, deprived of spiritual instruction, becomes mottled over with many a brand of sin. And our exercises here form a spiritual bath which, subjected to the warming of the Spirit, removes every uncleanness. Or rather, it is not merely the uncleanness itself, but even the color of it, which the fire of the Spirit removes. For, saith He, though your sins be as scarlet, I will make them white as snow."

Reading: 2 Kings 22:8-20; 23:1-8.

ROYAL LOVE LETTERS

He that hath my commandments, and keepeth them, he it is that loveth me; and he that loveth me shall be loved of my Father, and I will love him, and will manifest myself to him (John 14:21).
If ye keep my commandments, ye shall abide in my love; even as I have kept my Father's commandments, and abide in his love
(John 15:10).

Read and study the Bible as two young lovers read and study each other's letters. As soon as the mail brings a letter from his sweetheart, the young man grasps it and, without waiting to see if there is another letter for him, runs off to a corner and reads and laughs and rejoices over it, and almost devours it. If he is a particularly desperate and demonstrative lover—(the Lord make us desperate and demonstrative lovers of our Lord Jesus Christ!)—he will probably kiss it and carry it next to his heart till the next one comes.

Now, that is the way to read the Bible. It is God's will and testament. It is His own carefully written instructions as to what manner of people He would have us be; as to how we shall behave ourselves; what we shall do and not do; what our rights and privileges in Jesus are; what are our peculiar dangers; how we shall know our enemies and conquer them; how we shall enter into, and constantly enjoy His favor and escape hell and get safely home to Heaven.
—*Samuel Logan Brengle.*

> Our Father has sent you a letter from Heaven,
>   A letter from Jesus to you,
> To tell of His love and the home he's preparing
>   And what He expects you to do.
>
> At first you were thrilled and joyfully read it,
>   Perusing its pages with tears;
> But now it's forgotten—though just where you laid it—
>   And His voice has grown dim through the years.

Oh, seek His forgiveness and lovingly open
    Those beautiful pages once more,
That your robes may be white and spotless to meet Him
    The moment He calls at your door!

So carefully follow each word of instruction,
    Drinking in all of His love,
And He will forgive you, for there "it is written"
    In His letter to you from above.

And when you've been with Him up there through the ages,
    United with loved ones you've known,
You'll find all the glory He wrote on those pages
    And more—in your heavenly home!
—Alice Hansche Mortenson.

    The great cause of our neglecting the Scriptures is not want of time, but want of heart—some idol taking the place of Christ. Satan has been marvelously wise to entice away God's people from the Scriptures. A child of God who neglects the Scriptures cannot make it his business to please the Lord of glory; cannot make Him Lord of the conscience; a Ruler of the heart; the Joy, Portion, and Treasure of the soul.—*Robert Chapman.*

Reading: John 14.

THE AGELESS BOOK

Remember the former things of old: for I am God, and there is none else; I am God, and there is none like me, Declaring the end from the beginning, and from ancient times the things that are not yet done, saying, My counsel shall stand (Isa. 46:9-10).
This shall be written for the generation to come: and the people which shall be created shall praise the Lord (Psa. 102:18).

Whatever use man makes of this standard of truth, the standard itself remains fixed, tried and unimpaired. When I take down a great author, such as Lord Bacon, I find that time has discovered many errors, and rendered obsolete many positions to be found in that most comprehensive of human minds. But I see that time can take nothing from the Bible. I find it a living monitor. Like the sun, it is the same in its light and influence to man this day as it was ages ago. It can meet every present inquiry; it can console under every present loss, and it can become, in God's hand, a daily exciting cause of growth and comfort.—*Cecil*.

A short time ago a Bible seller in Syria was dragged off to the local police court for selling what appeared to be highly inflammatory political propaganda. The judge examined these strange books carefully and then demanded, "Where is that man Paul who wrote this book to the Romans? Bring him into this court!"

The Bible seller did his best to explain to the judge that the apostle Paul died almost two thousand years ago. The judge was slow to be convinced, but finally said to the Bible seller, "Here, you sign a statement declaring that you will be personally responsible for everything written in this book to the Romans. This document is too contemporary and its significance too timely not to have someone personally responsible for its contents."

The Spirit gives reality to the Old Testament, the prophetic record; and to the New Testament, the historic record of Christ's life. He impresses upon us the fact that Jesus is living and present—and that He is what He was. His birth, His sermon on the mount, His parables, His miracles, His words on the cross, to Spirit-illuminated souls do not belong to a distant antiquity, but are perpetually as fresh as the morning paper. The Spirit telegraphs the Gospel across the chasm of centuries and millenniums as recent news from Heaven.

"What are you so greedily reading, Grandpa?" said a child to a Bible-studying saint of four-score years, intently reading the Word of God. "News," was the reply.—*Daniel Steele.*

Robert Murray McCheyne once sent a Hebrew Bible as a present to a fellow laborer in Dundee, with the following lines:—

> Anoint mine eyes, O holy Dove!
> That I may prize this Book of love.
>
> Unstop mine ear, made deaf by sin,
> That I may hear Thy voice within.
>
> Break my hard heart, Jesus, my Lord,
> In the inmost part hide Thy sweet Word.

Reading: Isaiah. 51:1-16; Psalms 2.

ROYAL FELLOWSHIP

If ye abide in me, and my words abide in you, ye shall ask what ye will, and it shall be done unto you (John 15:7).
And the Lord spake unto Moses face to face, as a man speaketh unto his friend (Exod. 33:11).

It is a mistake to suppose that prayer alone is sufficient to nourish our spiritual life. Really it is only half of the communion with God through which we get the refreshing our souls need. A heathen convert said: "When I pray I talk to God; when I read my Bible God talks to me." Now it is just as needful to have God talk to us as it is for us to talk to Him. Yet we are not urged half so frequently or half so earnestly to read our Bible as part of our daily spiritual feeding, as we are to pray. There are many people who rarely ever carry the Bible with them into the closet. They drop on their knees a few moments in the morning and implore God's blessing on them for the day, and then they are up and away, carrying no word of God in their hearts as they enter the day's strife and toil. Really they have had only half a meal, and are not prepared as they might have been for duty. They should also have eaten some of the words of God, and then they would have been truly invigorated and made strong for their day's pilgrimage.—*J. R. Miller.*

> The counsels of redeeming grace
> The sacred leaves unfold;
> And here the Savior's lovely face
> Our raptured eyes behold.
>
> Here light descending from above
> Directs our doubtful feet;
> Here promises of heavenly love
> Our ardent wishes meet.
> —*Samuel Stennett.*

"He shall take of mine, and shall show it unto you," said Jesus. Here is one side—the communication of the life and love and joy of the Lord to us. "The Spirit maketh intercession for us." Here is the other side—the communication of our needs and sorrows, our praises and confessions to the Lord. And both these ideas are involved in full communion with Christ.

To establish this fellowship we make use, first of all, of the Scriptures, which are the inspired organ of the Holy Ghost. And it is very important for us to see that the most direct and intelligible means of communion is the Word of God. Thought, like the vine, needs a trellis on which to climb, in order to mount up into the sunlight. We require God's Word as a support and uplift in order that we may think God's thoughts after Him. And we are sure that the most substantial and most satisfactory intercourse which we can have with the Lord is attained in this way.—*A. J. Gordon.*

If you would learn the secret of power and usefulness and love—read the stories of God's giants in the Bible. Notice their lives are filled with two-way conversation—petitions on the part of the suppliant, and the ever-willing reply from God the Father, promising encouragement, denouncing sin, directing their pathway and revealing His own great almightiness. "And the Lord talked with Moses . . . And Moses said unto the Lord . . . And the Lord said unto Moses."

Reading: Exodus 33.

THE BIBLE—A DANGEROUS BOOK

Then cometh the devil, and taketh away the word out of their hearts, lest they should believe and be saved (Luke 8:12).
And he (the serpent) said unto the woman, Yea, hath God said . . .
(Gen. 3:1)?

God's Word is dangerous. At least Satan thinks so. The devil first attempted to deceive man by divesting God's Word of its truth, and therefore its power. In the Parable of the Soils (the Sower), the seed was not allowed to remain exposed even on the wayside—**The devil taketh away the word . . . lest they should believe and be saved.** Anything that deprives men of the Word, that dilutes its truth, that denies its authority, is devilish.—*G. E. Failing.*

In a large city of the United States a battle is being waged. It is over the posting of the Ten Commandments in the classroom as a moral code. It is possible to post the wisdom of Socrates, Confucius, Voltaire and even Karl Marx, but God's good code of living is denied a place. Why? It is the greatest compliment paid to the Old Testament that, after generations, authorities fear the power of the ancient Word on modern youth.

We may have come to take "liberal" views of the Bible, till we hardly know what it is to approach it except as its critics. Yet on a sudden this Book turns upon us, rises as it were in new and awful life from the dissecting table, and speaks to us with even more than its old authority about temperance, righteousness, and judgment to come, till we tremble all through.—*Bishop Moule.*

Thou hearest the Word, and thou canst in no way escape from it. Thou mayest deny it; but that will not kill it. Thou mayest try to shake it from thee; but it will not leave thee. Thou mayest bury it in the dust; but it will thence rise again. Thou mayest inter it in the grave of forgetfulness; but know that, like a specter, it will yet meet thee.

Thou canst never free thyself from the Word of God, if thou hast at any time come in contact with it. Thou mayest shut thine eyes, that thou see it not; but know that it will follow thee still. It accompanies thee as a silent companion; but, silent though it be, it is a dangerous companion.

Israel I. Saxe, writing in *The Jewish Era,* testifies: "I remember I burned about six New Testaments, but the seventh one burned me. When I received the seventh New Testament I decided to read it for the sake of education only. I at first struggled against the prejudice of the name Jesus Christ. Then I took a large sheet of paper and marked down all the Old Testament Messianic prophecies I could remember, and I also read the Old Testament that I might be sure I had all the Old Testament promises of the Messiah. Then I compared their fulfillment in the New Testament. After doing this I could not help but accept Jesus as the Messiah."

> A thousand hammers keen
>   With fiery force and strain,
> Brought down on it in rage and hate,
>   Have struck this gem in vain.
>
> It standeth and will stand,
>   Without or change or age,
> The word of majesty and light,
>   The Church's heritage.
> —*Horatius Bonar.*

Reading: John 8:26-59.

THE NEVER-FAILING PROMISES

For all the promises of God in him are yea, and in him Amen
(2 Cor. 1:20).
She judged him faithful who had promised (Heb. 11:11).
He staggered not at the promise of God (Rom. 4:20).

All the earth-born or devil-breathed fogs and clouds of doubt, from the fall until this hour, have not been able to touch the splendor of one star that He has set in the unassailable firmament of His eternal truth.

All the promises of God are yea and Amen—where?—"in Him," the Son of God. He holds these stars in His right hand; He has held the great promise of eternal life for us since God gave it to Him for us before the world began, and every other is sub-included. And it is one of His offices "to confirm the promises." Signed, sealed, held, and confirmed thus, should not "It is written" be enough for our present "light, and gladness and joy, and honor?"

> Then, exceeding great and precious
>   Are Thy promises Divine,
> Given by Christ, and by the Spirit
>   Sealed with sweetest "All is Thine!"
>
> Precious in their peace and power,
>   In their sure and changeless might,
> Strengthening, comforting, transforming;
>   Suns by day and stars by night.
>   —*Frances Ridley Havergal.*

Promises cover the whole period of human life. They meet us at our birth; they cluster about our childhood; they overhang our youth; they go in companies into manhood with us; they divide themselves into bands and stand at the door of every possible experience. Therefore there are promises of God to the ignorant, poor, oppressed, discouraged, etc.; to every affection, to every sphere of duty, to all perils and temptations. There are promises for joy, sorrow, victory, defeat, adversity, prosperity, etc. Old age has its garlands as full and fragrant as youth. All men, everywhere, and always—have their promises of God. They belong to mankind. There have been periods when, for special and beneficent reasons, God's promises seemed to belong only to His own people. And they are fresh with everlasting youth. The stars never wear out; the sun is not weary from the number of years. The heaven and the earth, however, shall pass away, but God's Word shall not pass away. Not one promise has ever been unfulfilled. There is not a witness in God's universe that can testify that he has leaned on a promise of God, and that God forgot to be gracious to him.—*Henry Ward Beecher.*

What can be more conclusive on this subject than these few lines by the hymn-writer, Lanta Wilson Smith?

> So I pave the path before me with the promises of God:
> They have brightened every step my feet have trod;
> And this shining, happy way brightens into perfect day,
> Through the never-failing promises of God.

Reading: Galatians 3:14-29; Romans 4:18-25;
       Hebrews 6:9-20.

SOUL FURNISHING UNLIMITED

All Scripture is given by inspiration of God, and is profitable for doctrine, for reproof, for correction, for instruction in righteousness: That the man of God may be perfect, throughly furnished unto all good works (2 Tim. 3:16-17).
Whatsoever things were written aforetime were written for our learning; that we through patience and comfort of the scriptures might have hope (Rom. 15:4).

    Here is a manual which describes the restoring means of grace. And if you know, in the circle of your associates, a man who is broken in will, or in hope or in faith, may I urge you to open this Book for him? He will find an abundance of hope, or infinite hope. Or if you are broken and here today with damaged wings, and you cannot soar, and are like a bird that has lost its power to fly, there are counsels here by which you can be made whole again. Try it, man, try it, and tell me how it goes.

    My last word is this: It is profitable for teaching, profitable for reproof, profitable for re-erection. This glorious word that backs up the whole task that the man of God may be complete: "furnished throughout." Not only profitable for regaining health, but for keeping it when you are furnished completely. It is almost audacious! It claims there is everything in this Book, everything you are going to need and every kind of crisis you are going to meet along the challenged road.

    Furnished completely. No need to go anywhere, for here there is counsel, direction, sure, definite, clear, by which you may be equipped to meet the lion when he leaps upon you from the thicket; to meet the snare in the road; to meet Apollyon as he straddles across the path; to meet death; to meet judgment—furnished completely.—*J. H. Jowett.*

> When sorrows come like shocks of doom,
> Or faith lies shattered in the gloom;
> When phantoms rise to block your way,
> And hopes are turned to somber gray
>   Give me one Book—Love's Book—the Bible.

When faith is strong and skies are clear,
When joy exults and laughs through tears,
When all the world is redolent
With choicest blessing heaven-sent,
   Give me one Book—Joy's Book—the Bible.

When sunset glow has fringed life's skies,
And time and toil have dimmed these eyes,
When for me comes the Pilot's call,
E'en then before the curtains fall—
   Give me one Book—God's Book—the Bible!
                              —*Unknown.*

   I do not set myself as an example, but I have spent ten times as much time over this Book as over all the other books in the world and have studied it carefully for over fifty years. I use it far more now than ever I did, and find more to enthrall the attention and affections than ever I did. I have never known one solitary emergency come to me that was not answered by this Book. I defy any man on earth to find an emergency in his personal life, domestic life, church life, business life that he does not find considered in this Book. All we have to do is to know this Book and it is a great shame that we do not know it better.—*A. T. Pierson.*

   Reading: Psalms 119:129-144; Psalms 119:161-168.

ABLE TO BUILD YOU UP

This book of the law shall not depart out of thy mouth; but thou shalt meditate therein day and night, that thou mayest observe to do according to all that is written therein: for then thou shalt make thy way prosperous, and then thou shalt have good success (Josh. 1:8). *I commend you to God, and to the word of his grace, which is able to build you up* (Acts 20:32).

Think of the Bible as a great spiritual dynamo releasing light, heat and energy.—*John R. Mott.*

Oh, you may talk about power; but, if you neglect the one Book that God has given you as the one instrument through which He imparts and exercises His power, you will not have it. You may read many books and go to many conventions and you may have your all-night prayer meetings to pray for the power of the Holy Ghost; but unless you keep in constant and close association with the one Book, the Bible, you will not have power. And if you ever had power, you will not maintain it except by the daily, earnest, intense study of that Book. **Ninety-nine Christians in every hundred are merely playing at Bible study; and therefore ninety-nine Christians in every hundred are mere weaklings, when they might be giants, both in their Christian life and in their service.**

There can be no fullness of life and service if the Bible is neglected. In much that is now written on power this fact is overlooked. The work of the Holy Spirit is magnified, but the instrument through which the Holy Spirit works is largely forgotten.

The result is transient enthusiasm and activity, but no steady continuance and increase in power and usefulness. We cannot obtain power, and we cannot maintain power, in our own lives and in our work for others, unless there is deep and frequent meditation upon the Word of God.—*R. A. Torrey.*

When I read Homer I'm sorry all men can't become giants. When I read the Bible I know they can.—*Frye.*

Mary Slessor's biography is still on the book-shelves of our shops today. Alone, and in the heart of the African jungle, her achievements and perseverance under all kinds of difficulties were a marvel. "Her own reading of the Bible was done early in the morning, as soon as it was light, generally about 5-30 a.m., when she took a fine pen and her Bible and turned to the book she was studying in the Old or New Testament. She underlined the governing words and sentences as she went along in her endeavor to grasp the meaning of the writer and the course of his arguments. Sometimes it would be three days before she would leave a chapter, but she did not leave it until she had some kind of idea as to its purpose, and then she filled the margins with her comments and became her own commentator."

A well-thumbed Bible will do mightier exploits than all the learning the schools can give.—*Smellie.*

A neglected Bible means a starved and strengthless spirit, a comfortless heart, a barren life, and a grieved Holy Ghost. If the people who are perpetually running about to meetings for crumbs of help and comfort, would only stay at home and search their Bibles, there would be more happiness in the Church and more blessing in the world. It is prosaic counsel, but it is true.—*F. B. Meyer.*

Reading: Joshua 1.

THE WONDER OF THE BOOK

They all wondered at the gracious words which proceeded out of his mouth (Luke 4:22).
They were astonished at his doctrine: for his word was with power (Luke 4:32).
They were all amazed...saying, What a word is this! (Luke 4:36).

One thing also I would add here, and that is my testimony to the wonder which the Book often excites in me. I could stop when I am reading it sometimes and cry over it. It is not that I understand it. Often it is because I cannot understand it that my wonder makes me admire. You can get to the end of other books. You have spent them out when you have read them two or three times; but you have only begun with the Bible when your hair turns gray. It is marvelous how wonderful the Bible is the first time you come to it. I think I almost wish I had never read it, that I might have the pleasure of reading it for the first time.—*C. H. Spurgeon.*

ALL DIFFICULTIES CANNOT BE SOLVED.—
They are too wise who are not content sometimes to wonder.
—*May.*

As I read my soul is conscious
   Of a tender, deep surprise;
Nor from bitter fonts of sorrow
   Gush the drops that dim these eyes.
Holy Volume! Take the tribute
   Which my tearful joy supplies.

...A week ago, I preached to a great congregation in Manchester Cathedral on Psalm 119:129 *Mirabilia* (wondrous things). I dwelt on the Bible, from the side of its inherent wonder, that mystery which no speculation can ever dissipate, the marvel of a Book which took at the very least 1,000 years and 1,000 authors to construct, under all imaginable differences of character, condition and period, and yet is found, by the human heart in every land and tongue, to be not half so much a Library as a Book, a living thing, one, with one soul and one message; above all, instinct with the presence and power of one Person. I am more and more impressed by the profound evidential and faith-confirming value of thus viewing the Bible as Many in one, One in many. It is in the strictest sense super-human—as a mere matter of observable fact. So I appealed to my hearers to approach the Bible *de novo* with the consciousness of its being a *wonder* before our eyes, and, if sure of that, to put in practice the maxim, "Let not what you know be shaken by what you don't know," and to interrogate it with renewed confidence for its message to soul and to life.—*Bishop Moule.*

Sadhu Sundar Singh, the godly evangelist, places the Bible high in his estimation: "In reading the Bible, I have found untold and eternal wealth of riches, such as I never thought nor dreamt before; and now in passing on its message to others, and sharing it with them, its blessing to me and to them continually increases. People can see the Book and its readers, but its wonderful unseen power and force of attraction are only known by those who read it sincerely and prayerfully. Just as the magnet and needle can be seen, but the magnetic force which draws the needle to itself is hidden and unseen, so the unseen power of this Word of God draws sinners like me to the Savior."

Reading: Luke 4:14-49.

RUDE INVADERS

Till I come, give attendance to reading (1 Tim. 4:13).
He shall read therein all the days of his life (Deut. 17:19).
I taught them, rising up early and teaching them, yet they have not hearkened to receive instruction (Jer. 32:33).

An old man was taught by his minister to read. He learned quickly, and was soon delving into the Word of God. The lessons ceased, and some time later the minister called at the little cottage to find only the wife at home. "How's John?" he asked. "He's canny sir," said the wife. "How does he get on with his reading?" "Nicely, sir." "Ah," was the remark, "I suppose he reads his Bible very well now." "Bible, sir? Why, he's been out of the Bible and into the newspapers long ago!" Poor old John represents a very large "clan" of Christians who have long since made their way "out of the Bible into the newspapers." What a terrible shame it is when we forsake the "fountain of living waters," and mess about in the muddy pools of human thought! There we seek in vain that which will quench our thirst.

Dr. Duff, in asserting the "claims of the Bible on the attention of man," remarks, that, "if other books are allowed to occupy our reading and study, almost altogether, instead of being friends and allies of the Bible, they must be accounted as the rude invaders of the sacred territory, that would drive the Bible from its commanding station in the foreground of our intellectual and spiritual landscape. These are the sacrilegious spoilers that would usurp the province of a Book replete with incense and redolent with the fragrance of Heaven. These are the cruel monopolizers of time and attention, that would feed our immortal souls with the garbage of secular knowledge, and leave them to famish amid the plentiful supplies of the bread of life, and the water of life, fresh flowing from the fountain of paradise."

Read the Bible, and read it again, and do not despair of help to understand something of the will and mind of God, though you think they are fast locked up from you. Neither trouble yourself, though you have not commentaries and expositions; pray and read, and read and pray; for a little from God is better than a great deal from man; also what is from man is uncertain, and is often lost and tumbled over by man, but what is from God is fixed as a nail in a sure place.

There is nothing that so abides with us as what we receive from God; and the reason why Christians at this day are at such a loss as to some things is because they are content with what comes from men's mouths, without searching and kneeling before God to know of Him the truth of things. Things which we receive at God's hand come to us as things from the minting-house, though old in themselves, yet new to us. Old truths are always new to us, if they come to us with the smell of Heaven upon them.—*John Bunyan.*

> Men's works with empty chaff are stored,
> God's Scriptures golden grain afford;
> Reject the chaff, and spend thy pains
> In gathering up these golden grains.

Reading: Proverbs 1.

GOD'S PANTRY

When he had spoken unto me, I was strengthened (Dan. 10:19).
Thy words were found, and I did eat them; and thy word was unto me the joy and rejoicing of my heart (Jer. 15:16).

The Word of God is the food of the life of God. The Word of God read, marked, learned, and inwardly digested is essential to healthy, spiritual life. The blessed man finds his strength in the law of the Lord, and in His law doth he meditate day and night.

Think how the milk is fitted to the child, or meat to the strong man; how each nourishes the whole system, turning into blood, bone, nerve, muscle; how each strengthens every organism—brain, heart, lung, eye, ear, hand. So the Word of God is fitted to the life of God within us, ministering to every spiritual faculty; invigorating all the graces of our new life—love, joy, peace, long-suffering, gentleness, goodness, faith, meekness, temperance; so strengthening us that to do the will of God is a delight instead of a burden, as a strong man rejoiceth to run a race.

And picture a babe without milk—a puling, pining, wasting thing. So is the soul without the Word, a life that is a prolonged dying, without growth, without beauty, without strength! The churches swarm with these sickly babes of twenty, thirty, forty, fifty years, always requiring to be dandled and petted, and always needing to be looked after, crying for cordials and to be carried—of no use to any living creature, only a burden to everybody. They have never fed on the Word.

This feeding means much more than reading. SEARCH, MEDITATE—these are the words which direct us in its use. We need to get in at the life of the Word, and we need to get the Word into the life.—*Mark Guy Pearce.*

"Most people expect to feed their body at least twenty-one times a week, yet they don't feed their soul as much as a Scriptural sandwich once a day."

When Alexander Peden, one of the chief heroes of Scottish Covenanting days, was passing through Clydesdale, he met one whom he knew, and said to her, "How fares it wi' ye in these evil days? Is it well wi' ye?" "Aye," she replied, "it is well, better far wi' me than in the days lang syne. I get mair out of one verse of His Holy Word then I used to get out of the world, for He has flung aside the keys of His pantry, and bidden me tak' my fill (take all I need).

George Herbert, speaking of the Word as food, poetically says:

> Or, when he hungry is, for better food
>   To feed upon
>   Than this alone,
> If he brings stomach and digestion good:
>   And if he be amiss,
>   This the best physic is.

Hearken diligently unto me, and eat ye that which is good
(Isa. 55:2).

Reading: Isaiah 55:1-5; Ezekiel 2:8-10; 3:1-4.

IT WORKS!

When ye received the word of God which ye heard of us, ye received it not as the word of men, but, as it is in truth, the word of God, which EFFECTUALLY WORKETH also in you that believe (1 Thess. 2:1-3) *So mightily grew the word of God and prevailed* (Acts 19:20). *And the word of God increased"* (Acts 6:7).

A mechanic was called in to repair the mechanism of a giant telescope. During the noon hour the chief astronomer came upon the man reading the Bible. "What good do you expect from that?" he asked. "The Bible is out of date. Why, you don't even know who wrote it."

The mechanic puzzled a moment, then he looked up, "Don't you make considerable use of the multiplication table in your calculations?"

"Yes, of course," returned the other.

"Do you know who wrote it?"

"Why, no, I guess I don't."

"Then," said the mechanic, "how can you trust the multiplication table?"

"We trust it because—well, because it works," the astronomer finished testily.

"Well, I trust the Bible for the same reason—it works."—*Selected.*

What power, what life, what strange energy have I experienced in it! What a change hath it wrought in me! What lusts hath it discovered and mortified! What duties hath it convinced me of, and engaged me in! What strength hath it furnished me with! How hath it quickened me when I was dead in sin, revived my comforts when they were dying, actuated my graces when they were languishing, roused me up when I was sluggish, awakened me when I was dreaming, refreshed me when I was sorrowful, supported me when I was sinking, answered my doubts, conquered my temptations, scattered my fears, enlarged me with desires and filled me "with joy unspeakable and full of glory!" (1 Pet. 1:8). And what word could ever have wrought such effects but that of the eternal, all-wise, all-powerful God? And therefore upon His authority alone I receive it; Him alone I adore in it, Whose power I have so often found working by it.—*Owen.*

Robert Murray M'Cheyne, whose church was visited with such a gracious out-pouring of the Spirit, began over thirty prayer meetings in different homes of his parish where the Word of God was read. This is what He says of the power of the Word: "'The Word of God grew,' and where that was so the following results appeared in believers: a feeling as if a second conversion was required; more love for the sanctuary; a holier living, giving up even doubtful practices, pursuits, and pleasures, leaving the company of the wicked, and avoiding all occasions or temptations to fall into sin. On the other hand, if the Word of God is not growing and not multiplying, then Christians become cold or lukewarm—Laodicean. Again, when the Word of God grows and multiplies, there are revivals of religion, notorious sinners are converted, and Christ's kingdom is advanced."

Reading: Acts 6:1-8; 19:8-20.

THE ROYAL PORTRAIT

The Word was made flesh, and dwelt among us (and we beheld his glory, the glory as of the only begotten of the Father), full of grace and truth (John 1:14).

If this Book were of man, the marvel would be too great; the only thing that causes our wonder to cease is the knowledge that it is the handwriting of the Living God. Yet men could not read that handwriting until He came Who is the Sum and Substance, the Center and Circumference of the Book, whose Divine Personality, in all His glorious perfections, lights up the whole Scriptures from Genesis to Revelation.

Take Christ out of the Scriptures and they lose all their meaning; study any portion without reference to Him, and the glory is all gone. Yet we must not fall into the error that some do, of depreciating the written Word and thinking that it is no longer needed, or that it occupies a lower place than Christ Himself. It is only through the Scriptures that Christ is revealed to us.—*H. D. Brown.*

It is well to remind ourselves of the close connection that exists between the written Word of God and the incarnate Word of God. We shall never enjoy the one apart from the other. It is through God's own revelation in the written Word that we really see and know the Word Who was made flesh and Who rose from the dead.—*Hudson Taylor.*

> I read Thy word, O Lord, each passing day,
> And in the sacred page find glad employ,
> But this I pray:
> Save from the killing letter. Teach my heart,
> Set free from human forms, the holy art
> Of reading Thee in every line,
> In precept, prophecy, and sign,

Till, all my vision filled with Thee,
Thy likeness shall reflect in me.
Not knowledge, but Thyself my joy!—
For this I pray.
—*F. C. Macaulay.*

The Bible is the Book of books, because it is the Book of God. It is my Guide and light, and Food for my soul. Experience has proved the fact that there is no other book in the world beside this, which can meet the spiritual needs of men. It is now about quarter of a century since this precious Book introduced me to its Author; and all this time I have found my Savior to be exactly the same as recorded in this Book. He has been to me all that we read concerning Him there. Language difficulties and textual criticism have not hidden its truths nor hindered in the least its life-giving influence in my heart, because of these words—"They are spirit and they are life."—*Sadhu Sundar Singh.*

"The Bible is written with a very different design from other histories. Other histories may be written generally to instruct or to amuse; but the Bible is written that we may know the God Who made us, and the God Who will judge us before we stand in judgment at His bar."—*Cecil.*

"But these are written, that ye might believe that Jesus is the Christ, the Son of God; and that believing ye might have life through his name" (John 20:31).

Reading: 1 John 5: John 20:26-31.

TRUST GOD'S INSTRUMENT

For my thoughts are not your thoughts, neither are your ways my ways, saith the Lord. For as the heavens are higher than the earth, so are my ways higher than your ways, and my thoughts than your thoughts. For as the rain cometh down...So shall my word be that goeth forth out of my mouth: it shall not return unto me void, but it shall accomplish that which I please (Isa. 55:8-11).
They know not the thoughts of the Lord, neither understand they his counsel (Micah 4:12).

Is it possible for a pilot to fly his plane upside down while he thinks he is flying right side up? The question was asked of an experienced jet pilot. He explained that such a thing is possible because the little hairs in the inner ear that aid one's sense of balance can become disturbed, causing one to lose all sense of position or direction. A case was cited of a flyer heading straight down toward the earth, because he trusted his own sense of direction rather than his instruments which showed him his altitude and direction. He was only saved by word from another plane, "Trust your instruments."
So it is with us human beings. Our sense of balance and direction becomes disturbed by the multitude of opinions about us. That divine instrument, God's Word, will always set us straight, showing us how mistaken are our processes of thinking, and giving us true direction according to His thoughts which are so far above ours.
A godly missionary, A. N. Groves, brother-in-law to George Müller, tells us how he maintained a straight course heavenward:
"Sometimes my heart seems bewildered in the labyrinth of thoughts and difficulties that lie before me; it does seem so hard simply and fully to follow the Word of the living God. Most persons you meet will hardly look at even the picture of it; and if we will not, how can God fully bless us? For it must be His own ways, His own plans, His own principles, that He will honor, and not ours.

"Remember the old rule, to judge according to God's Word; let us be neither frightened nor allured from it; believe me, my dear brother, it will be the rock on which our battle with infidelity must be fought; therefore now learn to trust your sword, for it will cut deeply if well wielded under the power of the Spirit."

Jonathan Goforth, the well-known missionary to China, met with great unbelief while still a lad at school. He tells how the Word of God convinced and grounded him at this time: "My teacher was an ardent follower of Tom Paine. He persuaded all the boys in our class to his way of thinking. The jeers and arguments of my classmates proved too much for me. Suddenly all the foundations slipped. I was confounded! Instead of going to my minister or any other human aid, I felt constrained to take the Word of God alone as my guide. Night and day for a considerable period of time, I did little else than search the Scriptures until, finally, I was so solidly grounded that I have never had a shadow of doubt since. All my classmates, as well as our teacher, were brought back from infidelity, the teacher becoming one of my life-long friends."

> Thou truest friend man ever knew,
>   Thy constancy I've tried;
> When all were false I found thee true,
>   My counselor and guide.
> —*George P. Morris.*

Reading: Isaiah 55:6-16; Jeremiah 23:21-32.

EVERY WORD A NUGGET OF GOLD

There was not a word of all that Moses commanded, which Joshua read not (Josh. 8:35).
Man shall not live by bread alone, but by EVERY WORD that proceedeth out of the mouth of God (Matt. 4:4).
Thou shalt not go aside from ANY OF THE WORDS which I command thee this day (Deut. 28:14).

The Word of God is a mine of unfathomable wealth. It fully yields its soul-enriching treasures to the search of the diligent, while it leaves "poverty enough" to him that deals with a slack hand.—*Storrs.*

They who study the Scriptures aright are like men who dig deep in search of metals in the bowels of the earth; they look for the bed where the metal lies, and break every clod, and sift and examine the whole, in order to discover the ore.

There is not anything in the Scriptures which can be considered unimportant; there is not a single sentence of which does not deserve to be meditated on; for it is not the word of man, but of the Holy Spirit, and the least syllable of it contains a hidden treasure.—*Chrysostom.*

> Each word of Thine a gem
> From the celestial mines,
> A sunbeam from that holy Heaven
> Where holy sunlight shines.
> —*Horatius Bonar.*

A perusal of godly biography convinces one that the man or woman God honors has always been one who loved, and deeply pondered His Word. Reginald Radcliffe, a Liverpool solicitor, was a well-known figure in the 1859 revival. A peep into his personal devotional life might give us a clue to his being so mightily used of God: "At this time the Bible, both Old and New Testaments, was very specially studied, without commentaries, but by taking subjects such as Prayer, Peace, the Holy Spirit, the Blood, Preaching the Gospel, etc. The Scriptures were searched from Genesis to Revelation, and not only chapter and verse written down, but the verses carefully copied, filling a large book of one hundred and sixty-eight pages. Mr. Radcliffe noted down that he had found the Bible an all-sufficient guide for his own heart and his life work."

John Sung was a Chinese evangelist who likewise experienced much of God's Spirit working with him in the salvation of souls. During his university course in the U.S.A., he was confined to hospital for six months where he had opportunity of studying his Bible. His biographer, Leslie Lyall, tells of this period: "He devoted almost all his waking hours to reading it through from beginning to end—which he did forty times! Each time he used a different scheme of study. And the more he read it the more enjoyment he derived from it. He seemed to be shown a key to the understanding of every one of the 1,189 chapters of the Bible. He made comprehensive word studies of a great variety of topics and recorded all his findings in numerous notebooks. . . . The Holy Spirit taught him much both through the Word of God and also in dreams and visions, material which he stored up in his mind and in his journals for future use."

A door is opened to you every time you apprehend one sentence or saying of the Lord's—a door in Heaven, shall we say? A door like that of which John speaks (Rev. 4:1), by which you are enabled in the Spirit to pass further into the secrets of God.—*Andrew Bonar.*

Reading: Nehemiah 8.

THE MOST MODERN BOOK

All flesh is as grass, and all the glory of man as the flower of grass. The grass withereth, and the flower thereof falleth away: but the word of the Lord endureth for ever. And this is the word...preached unto you (1 Peter 1:24-25).
All his commandments are sure. They stand fast for ever and ever, and are done in truth and uprightness (Psa. 111:7-8).

My conviction deepens that the Bible is the most modern book. It is the newest Book, just published, just out from Heaven and from God's heart. Our biography is in it. I have thought of taking this as a permanent text: "Is it not written in the book of the chronicles?" The modern newspaper is nothing but Moses and the prophets reproduced.
    The Bible is mysteriously divine, because it is mysteriously human. I see all kinds of people reading it, and every man finds it was written for him alone. Show me one phase of life that the Bible has not anticipated and addressed. It puts our thoughts into words; it fills our needs; and it teaches us the prayers that God can answer.
—Joseph Parker.

Do you want something old, something settled and sure,
That has stood through the ages and still shall endure:
Reliable records of all that is past,
Indelibly graven, forever to last?
Then come to God's Word and the message it brings.
The Book of Beginnings, first cause and first things,
Creator, Creation, a story sublime,
The darkness of chaos, the dawning of time,
The world that once was, and the world that now is;
Man made by God's hand, in His image, all His.

Do you want something modern and startling and new,
As fresh as the morning, as clear as the dew;

Today's current topics brought quite down to date,
Forecast of tomorrow that's never too late?
Then come to God's Word, for its prophecies hold
The symbols of all that the years shall unfold,
A wonderful outline of history's course
From a truly authentic and trustworthy source;
Naught else is so ancient, naught else is so new,
And nothing so wise is, and nothing so true.
While the vivid events of the past it can tell,
And the future's great drama is pictured as well,
Satisfying and full is the message it brings:
The Book of Completions, the end of all things.
—*Annie Johnson Flint.*

    A sea captain in the old days had a slave who sometimes steered his ship while the master slept. One night a star was pointed out by which the servant was to steer. The boat wobbled under the unskillful handling until the star appeared from behind. In panic he awoke the captain by shouting, "Massa! Come gimme 'nuther star: I'se sailed a-past that one!" We cry today that we are past certain old standards, for example, the Bible. It is because we have shifted, and are sailing in the wrong direction. The standards and the star are fixed; they are still far ahead of us.

Reading: Revelation 22:1-21; Psalms 11.

OBEYING ROYAL INSTRUCTIONS

Be ye doers of the word, and not hearers only (James 1:22).
Whatsoever he saith unto you, do (John 2:5).

    I believe the one chief reason that I have been kept in happy useful service is that I have been a lover of Holy Scripture; and I love it more now than I ever did.

    It has been my habit to read the Scriptures through four times a year; and it is important to read in a prayerful spirit, to meditate upon what we read, and to apply it to our own hearts. Do I understand this? Do I obey this? What has this word for me? Then, we must practice what we find in the Scripture; and the result will be a happy man, a happy woman.

    I have been for sixty-nine years a happy man; and I desire for my beloved brothers and sisters that they may be happy, happy, happy—ten times more happy than ever I have been in my life; for it is impossible to tell what God may give us in this way if we are thus lovers of Holy Scripture.—*George Müller.*

> Who has this Book and reads it not
>   Doth God Himself despise;
> Who reads, but understandeth not,
>   His soul in darkness lies.
> Who understands, but savors not,
>   He finds no rest in trouble;
> Who savors but obeyeth not,
>   He hath his judgment double.
> Who reads this Book—who understands—
>   Doth savor and obey;
> His soul shall stand at God's right hand
>   In the great Judgment Day.
>   —*Anon.*

A carpenter, when a companion questioned the correctness of some work he was doing on a building, pulled out a notebook and looked at it. "I am obeying instructions," he said. "I'm not the contractor, and I'm going by the book." But a little later, when he was ridiculing his friend for the latter's refusal to undertake certain work on Sunday, he was surprised to receive his own reply, "I am going by the Book. Someone else is responsible for the final outcome, all I have to do is to obey instructions. If that is the safest way to do when you are building a house, it is the safest way to do when you are building a life."—*"Forward."*

Study the Bible—to be wise.
Believe the Bible—to be safe.
Practice the Bible—to be Holy.

In keeping of them (the judgments of the Lord) is great reward
(Psalms 19:11).

Not, "Because I keep them I shall have a great reward"; but "*In* keeping of them there is great reward." God Himself wants us to keep them, because He loves us. He says: "O that there were such an heart in them, that they would fear Me, and keep **all my commandments always,** that it might be well with them!" This reward is an indisputable, though often not fully recognized fact of every Christian's experience. That we may have to keep His commandments in the very teeth of trial, loss, opposition, or distress does not touch the matter; for, nevertheless, not afterwards, but *in* keeping of His words, He takes care to keep His word that there shall be great reward.—*Frances Ridley Havergal.*

Reading: Deuteronomy 5:27-33; 6:1-12, 17-25.

IT'S GOOD TO SAIL BY

Thus saith the Lord, which maketh a way in the sea, and a path in the mighty waters (Isa. 43:16).
Thou shalt guide me with thy counsel, and afterward receive me to glory (Psa. 73:24).
O send out thy light, and thy truth: let them lead me; let them bring me unto thy holy hill, and to thy tabernacles (Psa. 43:3).

If you would know whether the Bible be true in its teachings you must go by it as you would by a chart. The chart is nothing but a piece of paper, and what good would it do for a half dozen captains to sit down on the shore and discuss its merits? How can they know whether its descriptions are correct or not?

Let them take it on board, and prove it, by sailing by it. It is a true chart which stands all tests and trials. If there is a rock where it says "rock," if it is safe where it says "safe," then it is a true chart, no matter who made it, or how, or when, or where it was made.

It is the sea that is the best test of a chart, and a human life is the best test of the Bible. Would you know the truth of the Bible? Become a Christian. "If any man will do his will," says Christ, "he shall know of the doctrine whether it be of God" (John 7:17).—*Selected.*

There is a chart whose tracings show
The onward course when tempests blow:
'Tis God's own Word! There, there is found
Direction for the homeward bound.

Give me this lamp to light my road;
This storehouse for my daily food;
Give me this chart for life's rough seas;
These healing leaves, this heavenly tree.
   —*H. F. Betts.*

The Bible is God's chart for you to steer by, to keep you from the bottom of the sea and to show you where the harbor is, and how to reach it without running on rocks or bars.—*Henry Ward Beecher.*

For a compass, chart and quadrant, God has given us the Bible; and most completely does it answer the purpose of all three.

By this Book, as a compass, you may shape your course correctly. It will always traverse freely, and it has no variation.

By this Book, as a quadrant, you may at any time, by night or by day, take an observation, and find out exactly where you are.

And in this Book, as on a chart, not only the port of Heaven, but your whole course, with every rock, shoal and breaker on which you can possibly strike, is most accurately laid down.

If, then, you make a proper use of this Book, mind your helm, keep a good look-out and carefully observe your Pilot's directions, you will, without fail, make a prosperous voyage, and reach the port of Heaven in safety.—*Edward Payson.*

I am a creature of a day, passing through life, as an arrow through the air. I am a spirit come from God, and returning to God: just hovering over the great gulf; till a few moments hence, I am no more seen! I drop into an unchangeable eternity! I want to know one thing—the way to Heaven: how to land safe on that happy shore. God Himself has condescended to teach the way; for this very end He came from Heaven. He hath written it down in a Book. O give me that Book!—*John Wesley.*

Reading: Psalms 107; Deuteronomy 31:9-26; 32:46-47.

ACKNOWLEDGMENTS

In seeking to obtain permission to use copyright material we have met with a most courteous and kindly response from publishers. We take this occasion to express our thanks in the following instances: Christabel Gladwell, The Bible and Testament Depot, for the poem by Edith E. Trusted, the quotation by Israel I. Saxe, and that from *The Message of God*; The China Inland Mission (Overseas Missionary Fellowship) for the quotations by Hudson Taylor and Fred Mitchell; The Epworth Press for the selections by Mark Guy Pearce; Beeston Evangelical Free Church Trust for the poem by Clara Simpson; The Evangelical Publishers for the poems by Annie Johnson Flint and Martha Snell Nicholson, gleaned from their periodical; the Editor of *Herald of Holiness* for the poem by Mrs. Alice H. Mortenson; Hodder and Stoughton Ltd., for the quotations by J. R. Miller and Sadhu Sundar Singh; Marshall, Morgan and Scott Ltd., for the writings of F. B. Meyer and the quotation by Jonathan Goforth; Moody Press, 820 N. LaSalle St., Chicago 10, for the poem by Ruthe T. Spinnanger and the selections by R. A. Torrey; James Nisbet and Co. Ltd., for the quotations by A. T. Pierson; Pickering and Inglis Ltd., for the poem by William Luff; Salvationist Publishing and Supplies Ltd., for the writings of S. L. Brengle; the editors of *The Sunday School Times* for the quotation by Armin R. Gesswein and the poem selected from their periodical.

Royal Counsel

By E. F. & L. Harvey

While preparing this book, the authors were so inspired by how much godly men and women attributed to their daily reading of the Bible that it completely revolutionized their study of God's Word. In reading its pages you, too, will gain a new sense of the importance of the Scriptures in your Christian life. *Royal Counsel* contains thirty-one two-page readings. Some of the titles are *Cargoes of Riches *Copyrighted in Heaven *Royal Love Letters *Soul Furnishing Unlimited *God's Pantry *The Royal Portrait *The Most Modern Book.

Other "Royal" Books

Royal Insignia
Ninety-eight readings on the believer's credentials of humility, brokenness, destitution, lowliness, etc. *208 pages*

Royal Pilgrimage
Thirty-eight readings to help to make earth a little less like home and heaven a little more so. *112 pages*

Royal Purposes
Thirty-one daily readings on God's purposeful dealings with His children. *64 pages*

Royal Exchange
Thirty-one daily readings on prayer—similar to Kneeling We Triumph. *64 pages*

For a complete catalog of inspirational literature, write to the address at the front of this book.

www.ingramcontent.com/pod-product-compliance
Lightning Source LLC
Chambersburg PA
CBHW031422040426
42444CB00005B/681